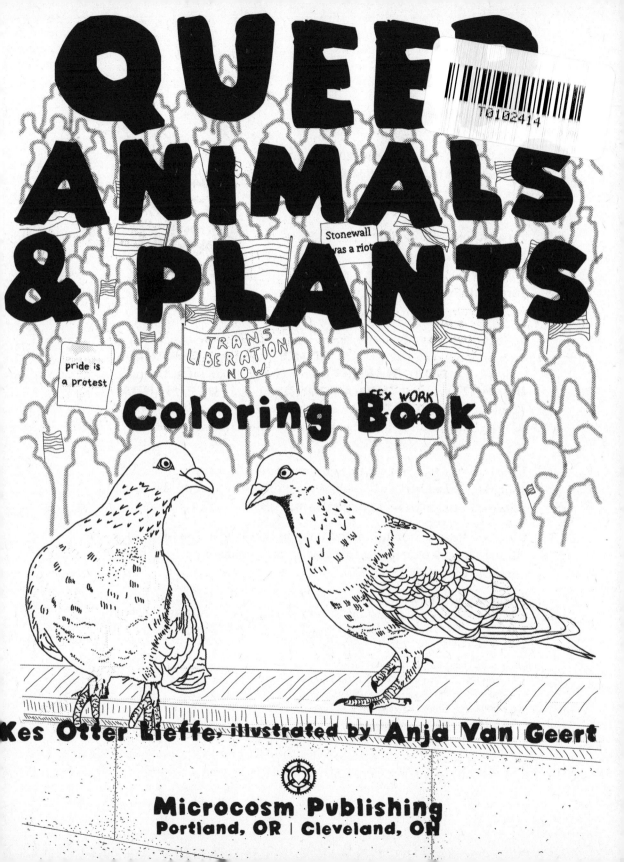

QUEER ANIMALS & PLANTS

Coloring Book

pride is a protest

Stonewall was a riot

TRANS LIBERATION NOW

SEX WORK

Kes Otter Lieffe, illustrated by Anja Van Geert

Microcosm Publishing
Portland, OR | Cleveland, OH

Queer Animals & Plants Coloring Book
© Kes Otter Lieffe, 2023
Illustrations © Anja Van Geert, 2023
This edition © Microcosm Publishing, 2023
ISBN 9781648411939
This is Microcosm #604

For a catalog, write or visit:
Microcosm Publishing
2752 N Williams Ave.
Portland, OR 97227
www.Microcosm.Pub/QueerAnimals

To join the ranks of high-class stores that feature Microcosm titles, talk to your local rep: In the U.S. **COMO** (Atlantic), **ABRAHAM** (Midwest), **BOB BARNETT** (Texas/Louisiana/Oklahoma), **IMPRINT** (Pacific), **TURNAROUND** (Europe), **UTP/MANDA** (Canada), **NEW SOUTH** (Australia/New Zealand), **GPS** in Asia, Africa, India, South America, and other countries, or **FAIRE** in the gift trade.

Did you know that you can buy our books directly from us at sliding scale rates? Support a small, independent publisher and pay less than Amazon's price at **www.Microcosm.Pub**

Global labor conditions are bad, and our roots in industrial Cleveland in the 70s and 80s made us appreciate the need to treat workers right. Therefore, our books are MADE IN THE USA.

A note from the illustrator:
In order to offer a realistic image of all the lovely animals and plants we mention in this book, I have worked with some amazing reference pictures. My main source for these pictures has been Pixabay and Istock photo, specifically:

Long-eared Hedgehog: iStock.com/EhayDy
Rambur's Forktail Damselfly: iStock.com/Timothy Loyd
Hooded warbler: iStock.com/psnaturephotography
Naked Mole-rat: iStock.com/GlobalP
Whiptail lizard: iStock.com/Christine_Kohler
Green Elysia Sea Slug: iStock.com/RibeirodosSantos

MICROCOSM · PUBLISHING

MICROCOSM PUBLISHING is Portland's most diversified publishing house and distributor with a focus on the colorful, authentic, and empowering. Our books and zines have put your power in your hands since 1996, equipping readers to make positive changes in their lives and in the world around them. Microcosm emphasizes skill-building, showing hidden histories, and fostering creativity through challenging conventional publishing wisdom with books and bookettes about DIY skills, food, bicycling, gender, self-care, and social justice. What was once a distro and record label started by Joe Biel in a drafty bedroom was determined to be *Publisher's Weekly's* fastest growing publisher of 2022 and has become among the oldest independent publishing houses in Portland, OR and Cleveland, OH. We are a politically moderate, centrist publisher in a world that has inched to the right for the past 80 years.

INTRODUCTION

*A*s a trans woman and an ecologist, I find queerness in non-human nature to be a profoundly important subject. There's something about knowing that there are lesbian lizards and kissing zebras that just gives me hope. Our queer communities can be a source of connection and can help us feel less alone, but what if those communities also extend way beyond human society?

Like many young nature-lovers, I grew up with wildlife programs and I never once heard about these things. As I began to research the few texts that exist on the subject, I discovered a world far richer than I could have imagined.

I have now been writing and teaching about this subject for years in my novels and workshops and realize more each day that none of this is new. While the term "queer ecology" might be relatively new, among Indigenous communities living closer to the non-human world than the industrial society I grew up in, this knowledge of more-than-human gender, sex and sexuality is ancient.

Queer is a word that has been redefined, reclaimed and debated like few others. As a queer activist for several decades, I have a lot of strong feelings about this word, political, social, personal. It's complicated.

In this colouring book, I've decided to play fast and loose with some definitions. Here I'm using queer as anything outside of those cis-het (and sometimes monosexual and monogamous and "vanilla" and non-intersex/dyadic) norms that biologists and wildlife documentaries have taught us to expect. I wouldn't necessarily use it this way to talk about human cultures. Queer is also often about questioning binaries and strict, simple categories. Non-humans do that too—a lot.

So for this colouring book, gay penguins are queer and polyandrogynous oystercatchers are, too. Intersex grizzly bears, binary-smashing lichens and also sex-changing willow trees.

Sex, defined by biologists, depends on the kind of gametes an individual produces— big ones or small ones. And nearly all sexually reproducing species have big and small gametes. "Males" produce small ones (sperm, pollen), "females" produce big ones (ovules, eggs). But some individuals produce both—either at the same time or during the course of their life (scientifically, species with a mix of reproductive organs, producing small and large gametes are known as hermaphrodites—not to be confused with the archaic word for intersex people). For plants, being reproductively both male and female is practically the rule rather than the exception.

Gender is also a thing and many species have multiple genders.

Animals and plants that are single individuals of one sex forever that only mate with other single individuals of another sex for the sole purpose of producing little baby animals and plants are actually pretty rare. As we'll explore in this book, sex is complicated, almost anything is possible, and we love that.

Again, I wouldn't necessarily use these definitions of sex or gametes when talking about human culture, I'm queer and trans, after all. But it's good to have some words, otherwise we could never appreciate the wonder of lesbian seagulls, sex-changing Yew trees, or multi-gendered parrotfish.

Although I'm aware of the dangers of talking about "intersex grizzly bears" or "lesbian lizards," I also believe that in this disconnected, alienated world, we probably don't anthropomorphize other species nearly enough. Any time we talk about other species, we run the risk of objectifying them—how could I ever really understand the experience of a parrotfish, nudibranch, or hedgehog? Gender identity is important for me, maybe it is for lizards too? How could I ever know?

I hope by bringing us closer to these other beings, we can gain more respect and empathy for their lives and a greater desire to protect them.

A quick note on "conservation status," while some species are labelled "least concern"—because that's what our research told us—apart from a few species that are doing exceptionally well, feral pigeons come to mind—I think we can safely assume that most species are living under some level of threat during this ecological crisis.

The point of highlighting "queerness" in non-human nature is also not to justify our existence as trans and queer people with examples from biology (although if you need to shut someone down who's claiming that queerness is "unnatural," then this book could definitely come in useful). This project aims to show that our beautiful queer community, human and non-human, is something to celebrate in all its gorgeous diversity.

This colouring book grew out of the *Queer Animals Coloring Book* zine which has been living its best life out in the community since 2020 provoking conversations and inspiring colouring-in parties. A copy even made its way to a display in a Queer Ecology exhibit in the Swiss (Bern) Natural History Museum. Considering that I imagined just such an exhibit in my 2018 novel *Conserve and Control*, the wonders of life and fiction blurring together have been tangible.

It is our hope that the format of a colouring book makes this information accessible to a wider range of people who might not pick up obscure ecology journals. As this isn't an academic paper, I haven't cited sources, but in case you want to do your own research, I highly recommend *Evolution's Rainbow: Diversity, Gender, and Sexuality in Nature and People* by Joan Roughgarden, *Biological Exuberance: Animal Homosexuality and Natural Diversity* by Bruce Bagemihl and *Entangled Life: How Fungi Make Our Worlds, Change Our Minds & Shape Our Futures* by Merlin Sheldrake. Learning more about this subject has brought me such joy, I hope this book can spark some of that curiosity in others.

All measurements in this book use the metric system because that is the primary unit of measurement throughout most of the world.

The beautiful illustrations of diverse animals—made by Anja Van Geert—bring the subject to life. We hope you share in this celebration with us by colouring in your favourite pictures with your loved ones. After all, at the end of the day, queerness is all about community.

Human, non-human. Natural, unnatural. Sentient, non-sentient. You, me.

Our intellectual world is full of binaries that are disrupted the closer we look at them.

I have maybe 40 trillion microbes living in my body at this moment—possibly outnumbering my "own" cells. Who am I?

The bacteria living in my gut can have viruses living inside them, and inside those viruses, other viruses. In Utah, a single quaking aspen tree has cloned itself to create a forest covering 43.6 hectares—it might be the heaviest known individual organism. And it is a forest. What are individuals?

94% of giraffe sex is between males. A quarter of tropical reef fish species change sex during their lifetime. There are whole species of lizards with no males at all. What is sex?

We hope you enjoy exploring these questions as much as we do. Welcome to the world of queer animals, plants, and friends.

QUEER ANIMALS

Homosexual behaviour has been recorded in hundreds of animal species beyond our own. Add to that the multiple genders, sex-changing, and intersexness in animal populations and the normative stories of wildlife documentaries are starting to look like a bit of a stretch. Some animals are famous for their queerness—bonobos for one, penguins for another—but the truth is that it is widespread among animal species and the more we look, the more we find. From damselflies to clownfish and from snails to mole-rats—queer animals . . . we love them!

AMERICAN BISON (Bison bison)

Found: North America

Size: up to 3.5 meters in length

Conservation status: of conservation concern,
  slowly recovering from near-extinction

This magnificent and critically important species has some queer stories.

Bison can be intersex. Some individuals have horns like males, external genitalia like females, and a uterus combined with testes. They bond with males and females. (Which is to say, non-intersex males and females, presumably defined by whether an individual produces small or large gametes during their lifetime. Words are imprecise tools sometimes.)

Some male bison like to get mounted. They actively invite penetration from another male by moving their tail and positioning their hips. Male-male mounting lasts twice as long as the straight average. Among bison, male-male mounting is more common than straight mounting, and large portions of the male population never breed. Female-female mounting also occurs from time to time.

Sometimes males form pair bonds together. They stay close, they have anal sex, and they defend each other. Bonded groups also exist—the same activities but up to four or five males.

The name researchers gave to these bonds? Tendings.

I know, it's perfect.

ANGLERFISH (family: *Ceratiidae*)

Found: all oceans from the tropics to the Antarctic, at depths up to 4km but mainly between 400 and 2000m deep

Size: females up to 1.2m, males up to 16cm in length

Conservation status: least concern

Okay, so these are pretty intense looking fish. They live in the deep and the dark and that little horn thing on their forehead? It's a bioluminescent light that lures in yummy prey. Which is already a lot. More unique than that though is their bizarre sex life. A male and female create a "chimaera"—a single individual with cells from different genotypes—think grafting an apple tree onto a different apple tree, but . . . fish.

A male finds a female using smell, then bites into her skin. He releases an enzyme that digests his mouth, and some of her body, until they fuse together. The male matures and while everything else atrophies, his testicles grow and they become a single fused hermaphroditic individual. Sometimes a few males attach to a female and they all become part of the whole, reproducing and living their best life.

For anglerfish at least, that's love.

BLUESTREAK CLEANER WRASSE
(*Labroides dimidiatus*)

Found: on coral reefs in the tropics from the Red Sea and Indian Ocean to the western Pacific (including Papua New Guinea, Japan, Fiji, and French Polynesia)

Size: average 10cm in length

Conservation status: least concern

We adore these little fish and you should too. Not only are they smart (studies show they might be the first fish known to recognize themselves in a mirror), they are exceptional service-providers.

Like other species of cleaner fish, these little wrasse live in symbiosis with larger, often predatory fish, setting up cleaning stations and grooming their clients for yummy ectoparasites (tiny animals living on the skin) and dead skin. They work a four-hour day and can service 2,000 clients in a shift. Sometimes they're naughty and take a little nip of protective mucus, but if they're being watched by other clients, they refrain. They have a reputation to uphold, after all.

And cutest of all, if a client gets annoyed with them, they can offer a fin massage reducing stress levels and repairing the relationship. They also offer this service to particularly scary predatory species, just in case.

But how are they queer? Like many other coral-reef species, cleaner wrasse are "sequential protogynous hermaphrodites" meaning they start life as females and later change sex to become males. Put two males in a tank and the smaller of the two can also shift back to female again.

And they're cute and smart and perfect.

BONNET MACAQUE (*Macaca radiata*)

Found: southern India

Size: up to 1.5 meters in length, with tail

Conservation Status: vulnerable

Like many primates, Bonnet macaques have a sexuality that's all over the map. Males mount each other up to four times as often as straight hook ups. They also jerk each other off, cuddle and mouth each other's necks. Females mount each other occasionally and sometimes "reverse mount" a male. Same-sex hook ups all like to rub their bums together.

They're also really into solo pleasure, using tools or even their own tails for stimulation.

Tails are handy like that.

COMMON SQUIRREL MONKEY (*Saimiri sciureus*)

Found: the Amazon basin

Size: around 1 meter in length, with tail

Conservation status: threatened by deforestation, the pet trade and medical research

Squirrel monkeys, like many primates, are pretty sexually active. But it isn't all about breeding.

A female sometimes faces another, tilts her head and makes a purring sound. Also popular are genital displays in which she spreads her thighs to show her vulva and engorged or erect clitoris. Then she turns, spreads her legs and presents her butt. Females also form friendships, travelling, resting, touching hands and kissing each other.

Males get into mounting each other too and sometimes get into a "pile up" of three or four climbing on each other to show their junk to their mates as a part of social communication. They also jerk themselves off and are flexible enough for auto-fellatio.

I know . . . they look so innocent.

DUNNOCK (*Prunella modularis*)

Found: native to temperate Europe and Asian Russia. Introduced to New Zealand

Size: up to 14cm in length

Conservation status: least concern

Rare among birds, Dunnocks are into polyandry: one female hooking up with two males. The two males have a strict dominance hierarchy between themselves. They work together to protect the territory and they both sing their gorgeous rapid, tinkling song. The female has sex with both of them.

Sex is fast—one tenth of a second—but they make up for it by repeating as often as a hundred times a day.

Depending on things like food, weather and territory size, Dunnocks can also be polygynous (two females, one male), polygynandrous (several females, several males) and even, occasionally, monogamous. They are very versatile lovers. Then, when winter comes, they spend a few months by themselves hopping around in bushes just coming together when there's something really interesting to eat. Some alone time is important in any polyamorous lifestyle.

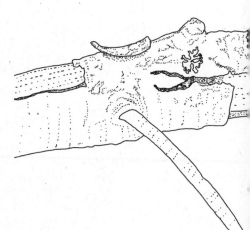

EURASIAN BLUE TIT
(Cyanistes caeruleus)

Found: Widespread throughout temperate and subarctic Europe and the western Palearctic

Size: 12cm in length

Conservation status: least concern

Blue tits are amazing little acrobats, often seen hanging upside down from bird feeders and tree branches in Europe.

Female blue tits sometimes pair up and nest together. Other species of birds also form female pairs but usually both lay eggs and have extra large nests. In the case of blue tits, only one female lays eggs and the broods are exceptionally small.

Blue tits have strange breeding behaviour in other ways too. 17% of straight sex occurs outside of the female's fertile season. About a third of females and up to a fifth of males form polygamous trios or even quartets. And overall, only about 15% of Blue Tits ever breed and about a third of parents never have grandchildren.

For many of us, Blue Tits are a very familiar little species but they have some surprising secrets.

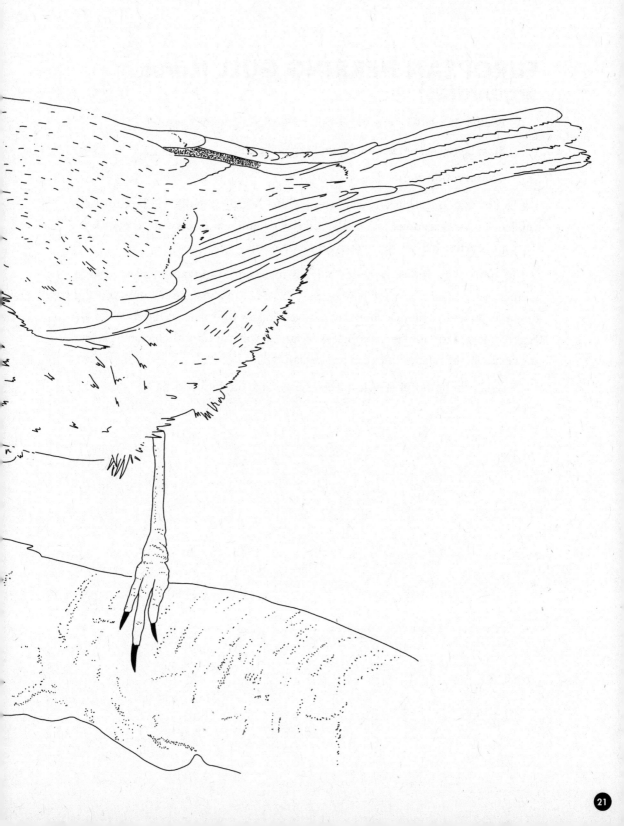

EUROPEAN HERRING GULL (*Larus argentatus*)

Found: mostly Western and Northern Europe along the coast

Size: up to 66cm in length, around 1kg in weight

Conservation status: least concern

For many Western Europeans who live near the sea, these birds will be extremely familiar. Loud, gregarious and really good at stealing chips, they are everywhere. They are also much gayer than you might have heard.

In some populations, same-sex couples make up 3% of all couples. Lesbian partners often build a nest and have eggs. If there's been a male in the mix, the eggs can be fertile and, as they can both lay, they can end up with an extra big clutch of 5-7 eggs (compared to 3 for hetero couples). Nearly all will pair up with the same partner the next year and relationships can be long-lasting.

Seagulls are beautiful seaside queers—just watch out for your fries!

GARDEN SNAIL (*Cornu aspersum/Helix aspersa*)

Found: native to the Mediterranean region and its present range stretches from northwest Africa and Iberia, eastwards to Asia Minor and Egypt, and northwards to the British Isles

Size: shell up to 4cm across

Conservation status: least concern

Snails. Gardeners hate them. Queer ecologists adore them.

Like all air-breathing snails and slugs, garden snails are hermaphroditic: they have a full set of sex organs and produce both sperm and eggs.

They also have an amazing—and slimy—sex life. In a two hour courtship ritual that can only be described as deeply romantic, two snails come together to tangle tentacles and attempt to stab each other with love darts. Yes, that's really what they're called. It isn't sperm—that comes later—but the darts do contain a chemical which greatly increases reproductive success for the snail who gets a dart in their partner. It doesn't always work and about a third of darts miss or fail to break the skin. Sometimes they get so deep in that they go through the head and end up poking out the other side. Intense.

But it works and if you've ever seen baby snails—tiny and transparent—you'll know how cute they are. Unless you're trying to grow some lettuce.

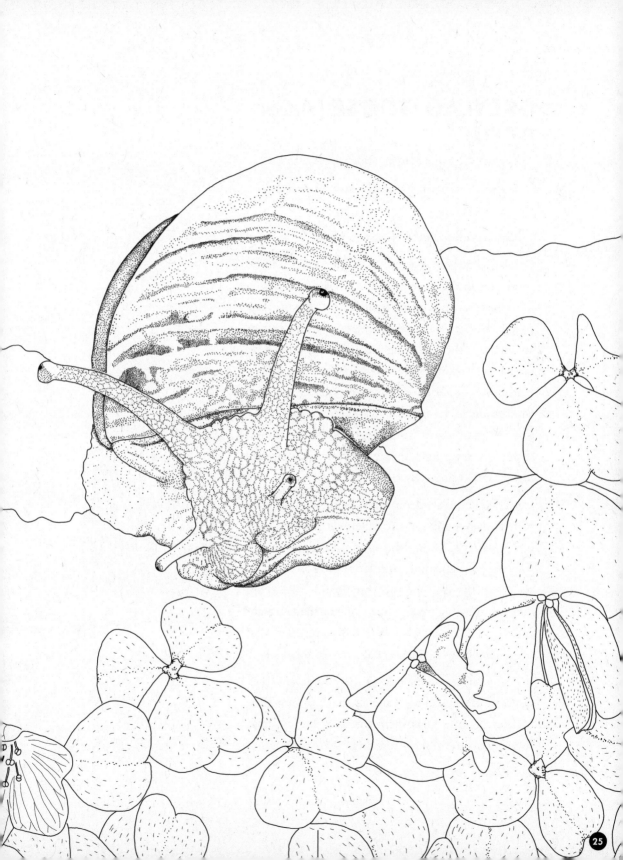

GREYLAG GOOSE (Anser anser)

Found: Widespread throughout the Palearctic

Size: Up to 91cm in length, average weight about 3.3kg

Conservation status: Least concern

Greylag geese can live up to twenty years and be coupled with the same partner for more than fifteen of those years. In some populations, 14-20% of those couples are between males (ganders). Gander couples are just as faithful as straight couples but quite a bit louder, performing duets and courtship dances. They mount each other often. Sometimes other males or females join in during sex and sometimes one of the pair will masturbate using a log. But the conclusion of any courtship and bonding is just the two ganders together; they are really close.

Their bonds are described as being stronger than male-female couples and a gander will grieve the loss of his partner. During the spring breeding season, gay couples spend time away from the hub of goose society, on the edge or away from the flock. As a pair, they are more aggressive and vigilant than straight couples and some researchers have suggested that these couples are acting as guardians for the flock.

Sometimes a female joins the couple and they nest as a trio. Or three ganders shack up together. Maybe a female joins them too and they all raise some fluffy little goslings together. There are options.

HOODED WARBLER (*Setophaga citrina*)

Found: North and Central America

Size: 13cm in length

Conservation status: least concern

Once upon a time there was a little Hooded Warbler called Y. Y was biologically male but did lots of things typical for female Hooded Warblers—like building a nest and sitting in it. Another male, called X, was into it and they shacked up and had some chicks together. Neither of them could lay eggs, but either a female had dropped some eggs off in the nest, or it was a sneaky cowbird—who lay their eggs in the nests of other species, like cuckoos do.

X brought snacks for Y and the nestlings. The nestlings were adorable.

Then tragedy struck. Their nest was predated. But, undeterred, the next year Y moved in with another male, Z, in a different territory and they built a new home together.

A true story brought to you by a single study in 1993.

Who knows how many other gender-switching stories there might be out there—for Hooded Warblers, and others?

RAMBUR'S FORKTAIL DAMSELFLY
(*Ischnura ramburii*)

Found: throughout the Americas

Size: 27-36mm in length

Conservation status: unknown

If you live in the Americas, you might have seen these gorgeous little damselflies dotting around lakes and ponds.

Females of this species come in two main kinds. One, a "heteromorph" is green or orange. The other, an "andromorph" is bright green and blue, just like the males.

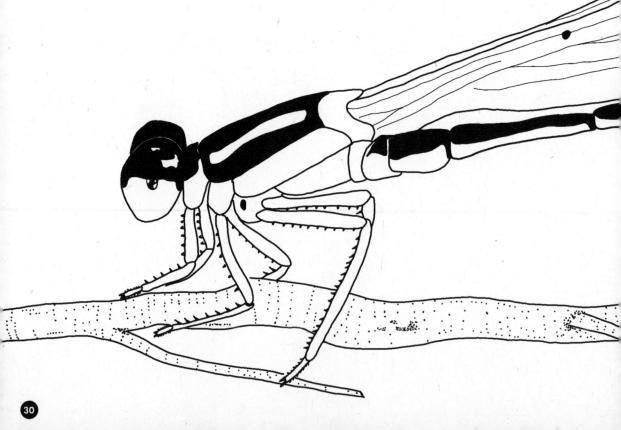

"Morph" just indicates it's about how an individual looks—adding "hetero" means it looks different, while "andro" means it looks like the males.

The andromorph females don't just look like males, they behave like them too. They also have a lot less sex. Considering that hooking up for damselflies takes three hours (and is a good time to get eaten by predators), and females only really need to mate once, this might be a big advantage.

Less is more if you're a transgender damselfly.

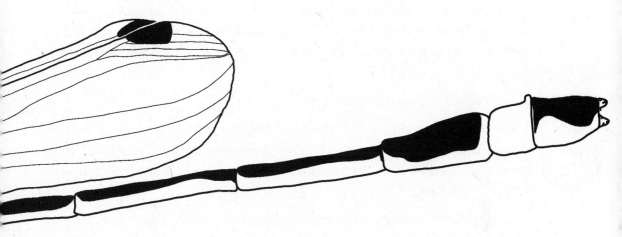

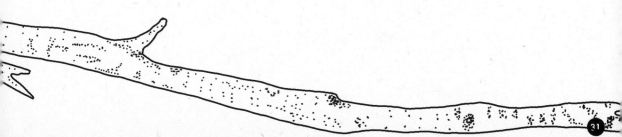

NAKED MOLE RAT (*Heterocephalus glaber*)

Found: tropical grasslands of East Africa

Size: typically 8 to 10 cm in length

Conservation status: least concern

Admittedly, naked mole-rats are pretty weird looking. They are also special in many other ways.

They live up to 32 years—longer than any other rodent—and create underground tunnel systems totalling up to five kilometers (three miles) long. They eat tubers that can be thousands of times their own weight and they also eat their own poop. Naked mole-rats can survive on very little oxygen, or no oxygen at all for a while—which is useful for living in tunnels. They lack pain sensitivity in their skin and have almost no cancer.

. . . Oh, and they're nearly all asexual.

Naked mole-rats, along with Damara-land mole-rats *Fukomys damarensis,* are the only two eusocial vertebrate species in the world, meaning they live in colonies—like some ants and bees—up to 300 individuals, with a queen and one to three sexual males.

The other 99% focus on things like tunnelling, protecting the colony and caring for the pups. No reproduction for the mole-rat masses apparently. Until the royalty dies or moves out and then anything is possible.

Are they cute? We can't decide. But they sure are fascinating.

SMALL FRUIT FLY (genus: *Drosophila)*

Found: worldwide

Size: mostly small 2-4mm in length

Conservation status: varies by species

Yes, fruit flies found their way into this colouring book. For anyone who has ever picked up a biology text book, you'll have heard of *Drosophila* sp. One species, *D. melanogaster* is considered a model organism in developmental biology and scientists are really into doing genetic research on them. Their genome was fully sequenced in 2000.

Males of one species, *D. bifurca*, have the longest sperm cells of any organism. Their bodies are just a few mm in length. Their sperm cells? Nearly 6cm when uncoiled—around 20 times larger.

And *Drosophila* gametes are interesting in other ways too. In some species, *D. pseudoobscura* for example, there are three sperm sizes—two small ones and one giant one. Which is pretty unique and comes dangerously close to shattering one of the only universal biological binaries—small gametes and large gametes.

Oh, and the females of this species are polyandrous and mate with several males.

You probably weren't expecting to read a story about fruit flies today.

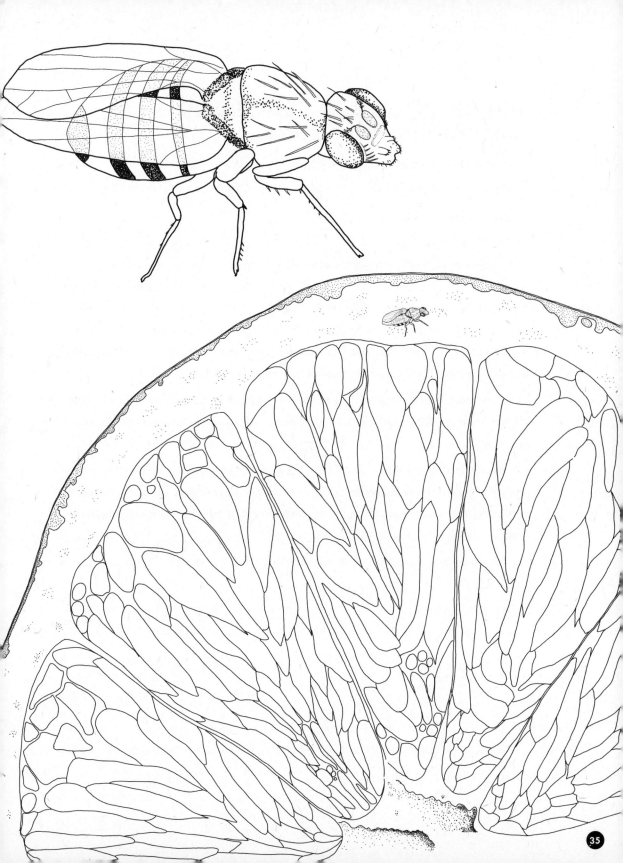

SOLAR-POWERED SEA SLUGS
(superorder: *Sacoglossa*)

Found: worldwide in tropical and temperate oceans

Size: varies by species

Conservation status: varies by species

When is an animal not quite an animal? When it photosynthesizes like a plant. Most plants make energy from sunlight using cells called chloroplasts. Animals, in general, do not. However these magical little sea slugs, unique among multicellular animals, take the chloroplasts from their algae snacks and incorporate them into their own tissues. And voilá, they become solar powered. It's something akin to us eating a salad and then incorporating salad super powers into our bodies so we could sit in the sun and photosynthesize and not have to eat as much.

They still prefer the animal way of doing things when possible, but they've been known to survive for months just on solar power—it's always good to have a back-up generator.

By the way, two species, *Elysia marginata* and *E. atroviridis,* will also decapitate themselves, their heads surviving without a heart or vital organs for nearly a month until they grow a new body. It might be a way to cast off parasites or evade predators, but for now it's a bit of a mystery. Also . . . wow!

Sea slugs—breaking binaries and making life more wonderful.

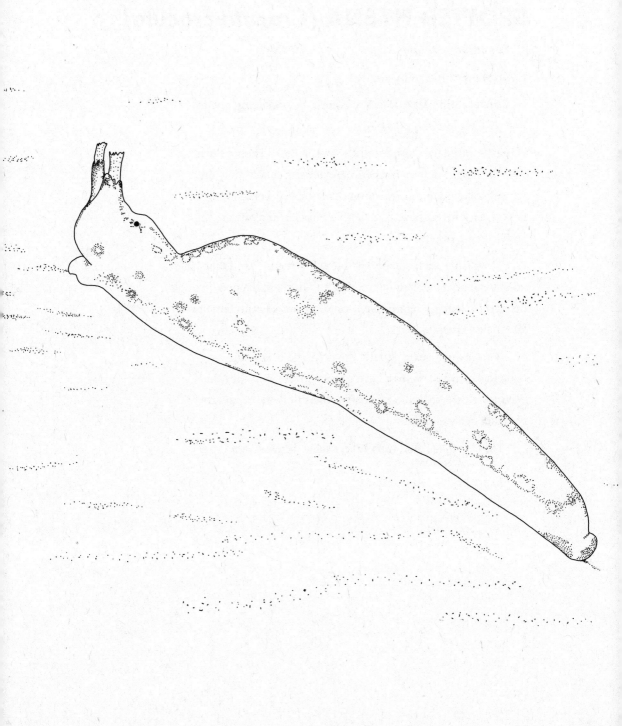

SPOTTED HYENA (*Crocuta crocuta*)

Found: sub-Saharan Africa

Size: up to 166cm in length

Conservation status: least concern, but declining due to
habitat loss and poaching

Female spotted hyenas have really special junk. Their clitoris is
90% the length of a male's penis and it can become fully erect,
which happens a lot in "meeting ceremonies." Females line up
next to each other, head to tail, lift a hind leg and nuzzle, sniff
and lick each other.

Their labia are fused into a "pseudo-scrotum" and they have
no vaginal opening. Peeing, mating and birth all happen through
the clitoris. And there are spines on the glans of both females
and males. Ouch.

For the guys, sex is usually the privilege of a single
male in a clan and the rest have to go without. But they find
ways to release, including thrusting their junk in the air and
spontaneously ejaculating.

The Lion King could have been such a different story.

WALRUS (*Odobenus rosmarus*)

Found: the Arctic Ocean and subarctic seas of the Northern Hemisphere

Size: 2,000 kg in weight

Conservation status: vulnerable, threatened by climate change

Walrus males enjoy each other's company. Especially when wet.

In shallow waters, they court each other by floating around in groups of up to 50, touching noses, rubbing against each other and sometimes sleeping together in a line, head up, tail down, clasping onto the walrus in front. They sing to each other, dive off rocks and sometimes jerk themselves off with their flippers. If things get really heated, two males will mount.

And they like it a lot—about a quarter of male social interactions involve courtship, snuggling, and sex and can take up 3% of the time they spend in the water. About 40-60% of sexually mature males choose gay sex over straight sex and many never breed. They mount and snuggle each other up to five times an hour.

Really though, who wouldn't want to snuggle with a walrus?

NUDIBRANCH (order: *Nudibranchia*)

Found: in seas worldwide

Size: varies by species, from 4-600mm in length

Conservation status: varies by species

I mean . . . how could we not include nudibranches? There are about 3,000 species of these often wildly coloured mollusks living in the world's seas. As their neon colour schemes suggest, many species of nudibranch are poisonous. They either generate their own poisons, or assimilate them from their toxic snacks. They're hermaphroditic and have a gorgeous courtship dance that could put any synchronized swimming team to shame.

Just gorgeous.

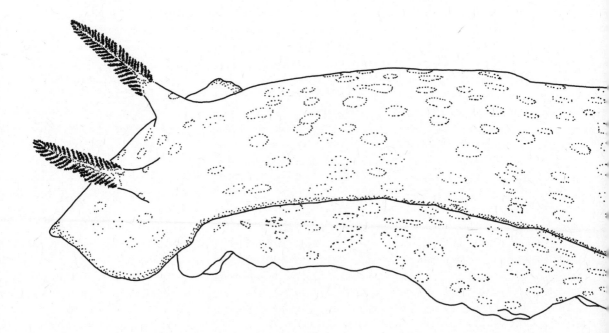

HUMMINGBIRDS (family: *Trochilidae*)

Found: across the Americas, mostly in the tropics

Size: varies by species

Conservation status: varies by species

You might think we included hummingbirds just because they're fun to colour in and it's true—they are stunning. But they also have a fun sex/gender story we know you'll enjoy.

Hummingbirds are fascinating in so many ways. Busy little nectar feeders, they include the smallest dinosaur known to have ever existed—the bee hummingbird (*Mellisuga helenae*), weighing in at just 2 grams (and yes, all birds are dinosaurs, it's a thing). Some species can flap their wings up to eighty times per second. And they are colourful, often iridescent—through pigmentation and cells that refract light, they can appear to change colour just by shifting position.

But that's mostly males, right? Like peacocks, hummingbirds have a high degree of sexual dimorphism—males and females look very different and in this case males tend to be flashy and females less so. Except that hummingbirds rock the binary in a big way. Males can look like females, females can look like males; it's a spectrum. In a study of 300 hummingbird species (there are 360 in total), 25% of species had females that looked like males, i.e., flashy, shiny, and all dressed up. There are various ecological and behavioural theories for why it happens—and with such frequency. Sex and gender are complicated for hummingbirds and we love them for it.

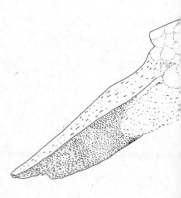

MALLARD (*Anas platyrhynchos*)

Found: across the Northern Hemisphere. Introduced to New Zealand, Australia, Peru, Brazil, Uruguay, Argentina, Chile, Colombia, the Falkland Islands, and South Africa

Size: up to 65cm in length

Conservation status: least concern

For many, mallards are the quintessential ducks, dabbling around in park ponds and feasting on stale bread thrown to them by enthusiastic admirers. What some of those generous humans don't know is that mallards love forming gay partnerships, sexual and non-sexual.

In early fall, as mallards gather in groups and start forming pair-bonds, some females get really into each other. They perform a super cute head bobbing display (called "pumping"), and they mount.

Drakes (males) form partnerships together, but it's generally non-sexual—swimming, resting, preening, feeding and (unconfirmed) snuggling in front of the TV. In some populations, up to 19% of all pairs are pair-bonds between two drakes. Sometimes a female joins them, and it heats up—both males might have sex with her, but their partnership stays primary and can last for years.

Taking a walk in the park some time? Bring some snacks (corn, peas, lettuce or grapes are better for them than bread) and spend some time hanging out with the queers.

KESTREL (*Falco tinnunculus*)

Found: widespread in Europe, Asia and Africa and occasional North America

Size: up to 39cm in length

Conservation status: least concern

You might have seen kestrels hovering over a field by the side of a road. They are spectacular little falcons with a super power—they can actually see near-ultraviolet. What shows up in near ultraviolet? Rodent pee, which certainly makes hunting a lot easier.

Kestrels are also very sexual. During the breeding season they might copulate up to three times an hour; as many as 230 times in a season.

Up to 10% of males have two girlfriends (sometimes each with their own nest) and a single female sometimes shacks up with two guys.

Male-male pairs exist too and they fly together with dramatic courtship rituals that bring them closer together for when they get back home to . . . chill.

Also, have you seen them hovering? Incredible.

CASSOWARY (*Casuarius* spp.)

Found: in the tropical forests of New Guinea (Papua New Guinea and Indonesia), East Nusa Tenggara, the Maluku Islands, and northeastern Australia.

Height: up to 2 m

Weight: up to 58.6 kg

Conservation status: the southern cassowary is endangered in Queensland

Cassowaries are surely one of the most magnificent birds on earth. Flightless and massive with a brightly-colored helmet used for crashing through forests, they also have a unique genital anatomy.

Most male birds in the world don't have a penis, but Cassowary males do. As it's involved in sex but isn't connected to internal organs, scientists sometimes call it a male clitoris. All females also possess a phallus which is basically the same, just a little smaller. On top of that, like other birds they mate and lay eggs through another orifice called the cloaca which, by the way, is also their anus.

Magnificent and pretty special.

GRIZZLY BEARS (*Ursus arctos horribilis*)

Found: Coastal North America

Length: up to 198 cm

Weight: up to 360 kg

Conservation status: least concern

Powerful, fierce, Grizzles are sometimes gay and intersex. Grizzlies are maybe a surprising addition to a book on queer animals, but they shouldn't be. Powerful, fierce, they are also sometimes gay and intersex. Females often bond for a few seasons raising cubs and defending food—even heading out into the cold and visiting each other during hibernation. One study showed up to 20% of females engaging in these companionships at some point in their life; sometimes involving three, four or even five female bears.

Some populations of grizzlies have a higher-than average proportion of intersex members - up to 25 percent in some areas. For grizzlies that means having genetics and internal reproductive organs associated with females, combined with a "penis-like organ". Most intersex grizzlies are parents and some give birth through the tip of their penis.

Now you know.

MUTE SWANS (*Cygnus olor*)

Found: native to Eurosiberia and North Africa. Introduced to North America, Australasia and South Africa

Length: up to 170 cm

Weight: up to 23 kg

Conservation status: least concern

For many, swans are the epitome of respectable, and straight, monogamy. We all know that they mate together for life and create ideal families.

That's not entirely accurate.

Mute swans are actually known to happily go off and create gay partnerships, both male and female, sometimes building nests and raising chicks together. Many are exclusively into same-sex hook ups, and non-breeding birds will gather into their own flocks seperate from the breeders.

But at least they're faithful, right? Nope. Some mate with other birds while still paired with their partner and some of these "flings" involve females mounting males. They don't even limit themselves to fun within their species and will get together with other kinds of swans and even geese. In the closely related Black swan, 14% of all bonds involve two males pairing with a female.

Maybe swans *do* represent family values for some, but they're probably not the values many would have expected.

LONG-EARED HEDGEHOGS (*Hemiechinus auritus*)

Found: steppes and desert of Central Asia and the Middle East.

Length: up to 27cm

Weight: up to 400 grams

Conservation status: least concern

Long-eared hedgehogs aren't super famous in the queer animal world. They're no giraffe, koala or dolphin. But they are incredibly cute. And super into oral sex.

A typical "lesbian interaction" according to the research begins at dusk. It starts with some cuddling and mutual rubbing and quickly escalates to sniffing, licking and nibbling each other's genitals. Sometimes a female will lift her butt in the air to give her partner better access. Sometimes they both do it to initiate mounting.

Heterosexual pairs are into it as well, but just to be clear, it's the male that sniffs and licks the female.

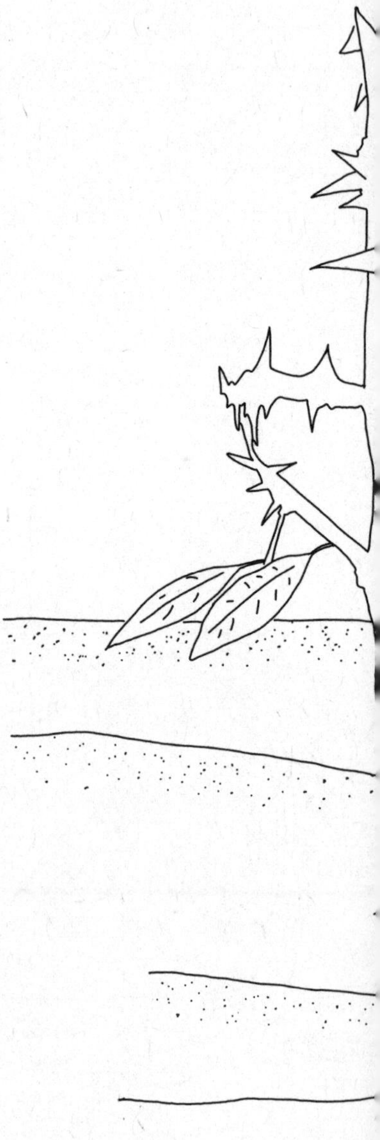

PARROTFISH (Several species, family: *Scaridae/Scarinae*)

Found: in coral reefs, rocky coasts, and seagrass beds particularly in the Indo-Pacific

Size: some species reach up to 1.3 metres in length

Conservation status: varied, depends on species

Parrotfish must be one of the most beautifully patterned and multi-colored fish in the sea. They're also sex-changing, multi-gendered, wonderfully complex beauties. Scientists call them "sequential hermaphrodites" as, along with 25% of coral reef fish species, parrotfish fully change sex, sometimes repeatedly during their lifetimes.

As for gender, striped parrotfish (*Scarus croicensis*) have such complex lives, they've been assigned five distinct genders based on if they've changed sex or not, the kind of genitals they currently have (biologists love that kind of thing) and their color. With multiple sexes and genders within one lifetime and plenty of fluidity between them, parrotfishes are as queer as they come. So much so that scientists needed a word for those unusual species who *don't* change sex, those with distinct sexes in which males remain males and females remain female. It's gonochoristic, by the way. You're welcome.

AMERICAN FLAMINGO (*Phoenicopterus ruber*)

Found: saline lagoons, mudflats, and shallow, brackish coastal or inland lakes.
From the Galápagos islands to the caribbean

Height: up to 145 cm

Weight: up to 2.8kg

Conservation status: least concern

Elegant, glamorous and outrageously pink, no-one should be too surprised that flamingos can be queer. Both males and females form same-sex pairs, feeding, travelling and sleeping with their partners. Female pairs apparently engage in "full genital contact" and male pairs build super sized nests to incubate, hatch and raise foster chicks. Sometimes they have no previous experience with different-sex partners and sometimes they're bi. One thing's for certain though, they are always fabulous.

BATS (order: *Chiroptera*)

Species: over 1,200 individual species, around 20% of all mammal species

Found: throughout the world, with the exception of extremely cold regions

Size: the largest species of bat can weigh up to 1.6 kg and have a wingspan of 1.7 m

Conservation status: varied, depends on species

Bats might not be everyone's favourite animal, but they have intimate, sexual lives and more than twenty species have been observed "engaging in homosexual behaviour"— from mutual grooming to cross-species gay sex.

Grey-headed flying foxes (*Pteropus poliocephalus*) of all sexes get into nibbling the chests and wings of their same-sex partners. Vampire bats (subfamily: Desmodontinae**)** perform fellatio on each other. Male Indian flying foxes (*Pteropus medius*) mount each other with erections while play-wrestling. Even Natterer's (*Myotis nattereri*) and Daubenton's (*Myotis daubentonii*) bats, two totally different species have been seen having gay fun together.

There are definitely some queer vampire stories to be told there.

KOALA (*Phascolarctos cinereus*)

Found: eucalypt woodlands in Australia

Length: up to 85 cm

Weight: up to 15 kg

Conservation status: vulnerable

Cute, cuddly and sometimes queer. Female koalas enjoy lesbian sex, and they love orgies. Some studies have counted three gay interactions for every straight one and up to five females might join in to have *very* noisy sex together. In their continued attempts to "explain" this behaviour, which seems to happen mostly in captivity, researchers have proposed that it could be some kind of stress reliever. Makes sense.

FERAL PIGEON (*Columba livia domestica*)

Found: towns and cities everywhere!

Length: up to 37 cm

Weight: up to 380g

Conservation status: least concern

Few birds are as familiar to city-dwellers around the world as the feral pigeon. Some love them, some hate them, but they are pretty much everywhere. You guessed it: they're queer. Both males and females create same-sex pairs, building nests together and having sex. If a male partner deserts a brood or dies, hens will sometimes pair up, lay eggs and incubate them.

Next time you see a flock of pigeons in a city square, just remember, humans aren't the only queers in the city.

WHIPTAIL LIZARD (*Cnemidophorus* spp., *Aspidoscelis* spp.)

Found: mostly deserts in Southwestern United States, South and Central America, and the West Indies.

Size: varies

Conservation status: varies

Rarely mentioned and often ignored as an anomaly or an evolutionary dead end (and haven't we all heard that before?), there are several species of lizard, at least eight in the south-west of North America, who are completely female. There is not a single male in these species and there is no need for reproductive sex: females produce fertile eggs all by themselves.

As we all know—because we've been told this lie since birth—animals only have sex to make little baby animals, so for a long time, scientists assumed these female-only lizards didn't, wouldn't, or couldn't have sex. After all, what would be the point?

They do. A lot. In fact, they follow a highly intricate courtship pattern and two females sharing a burrow and sleeping there together will cycle their hormones, one with high progesterone levels who becomes the top, and one with high estradiol levels who becomes the bottom. After a few weeks, they switch hormone levels and position.

Major scientific journals still refer to the whiptail lizards as "celibate" despite all the—great deal of—lesbian sex going on right in front of the biologists' homophobic eyes. Presumably, for some commentators at least, unless there's a male penetrating a female, there simply is no sex.

Interesting fact: studies have shown that compared with similar species that have both males and females, the female-only whiptail species are four times less aggressive and have a much less marked dominance hierarchy. Surprised? Didn't think so.

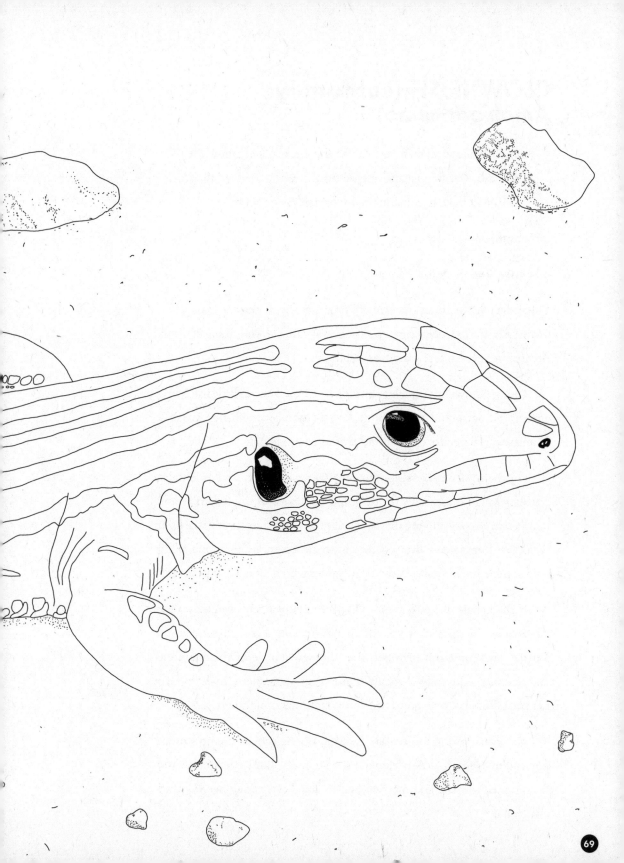

CLOWNFISH (subfamily: *Amphiprioninae*)

Found: shallow waters and reefs. Indian sea, including the Red Sea. Pacific Oceans, including the Great Barrier Reef, Southeast Asia, Japan, and the Indo-Malaysian region.

Length: up to 17 cm

Conservation status: varies

The more I learn about queerness in nature, the happier it makes me. Clownfish, for example, change sex several times during their lifetime. Because yes everyone, Nemo was totally trans.

Orange Clownfish (*Amphiprion percula)*, those famous little fish living among the poisonous tentacles of sea anemones can change twice—from asexual juveniles to male and from male to female.

For them, size confers dominance. Bigger is better. And as females are bigger than males, they're also more dominant. A single female and male form a cozy monogamous straight relationship (don't worry, it won't last forever) and live together in their poisonous anemone along with some differently sized asexual juveniles who float in on the current.

If the female dies or leaves (or like in the movie, gets eaten by a big barracuda), the male starts to buff up, put on weight and changes sex to female. That same fish then becomes the new female of the anemone and one of the juveniles sexually matures and becomes a male to take her place. And back we go to cozy monogamous straightness…

So, you know, in the realistic version of the movie, Nemo's mom got eaten, Nemo's dad became his new mom, and agender Nemo transitioned to male and married her. Really, I can't imagine why they changed it.

DOLPHINS (infraorder: *Cetacea*, 40 species)

Found: widespread, mostly warmer waters of tropical zones

Size: common bottlenose dolphins can measure up to 3.5 m and weigh up to 500 kg

Conservation status: varies

Dolphins are one of the most charismatic groups of animals in the world. From Flipper to Seaworld, they are adored by humans everywhere (except when being hunted, poisoned and incarcerated, obviously.) Little did we know that they're also total perverts.

Bottlenose dolphins (*Tursiops* spp.) are big into oral sex. Males and females alike will insert their snout into the genital slit of another, stimulating their partner and pushing them along in the water, just for fun. Scientists call it "beak-genital propulsion" by the way, which is pretty romantic. Males and females both enjoy other kinds of penetration too, sometimes from another dolphin's fin or tail.

Atlantic Spotted Dolphins (*Stenella frontalis*) have a particularly fun way to please each other, known as a "genital buzz." One dolphin can direct a sexy sound wave through the water, stimulating their partner. They're also sexually pursued by Bottlenoses—a totally different species—sometimes mating with two bottlenoses at the same time. Sometimes these pursuits are playful, sometimes aggressive. Scientists believe that these sexual pursuits may lead to cooperation on hunts.

They get even more creative than that. Male Botos (*Inia geoffrensis*) have been seen penetrating their male partner's blowhole—in the top of his head. That's pretty kinky.

Talkative, funny, beautiful—dolphins are many things. But vanilla certainly isn't one of them.

WEST INDIAN MANATEES (*Trichechus manatus*)

Found: coastal waters and rivers of southeastern US, the Caribbean and northeastern Brazil

Length: up to 3.5 m

Weight: up to 600 kg

Conservation status: vulnerable

These manatees are large aquatic mammals that live in the Caribbean, northeastern Brazil and the southeast of North America. Despite common assumptions about queerness in the

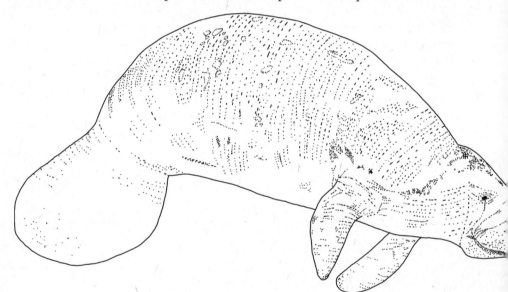

animal kingdom, these beautiful mammals are really very gay. Male manatees of all ages commonly engage in gay sex.

And it's a total party.

Two male manatees will sometimes begin sex by kissing their muzzles together above the water. They sometimes mate in a head to tail position, nibble each other's bits and masturbate each other with a flipper. All this is quite different to straight sex in this species and *generally lasts two to four times as long.*

Often males form orgies of up to four, kissing, thrusting and rubbing their dicks against each other. They have also been known to make uniquely gay sounds of pleasure, different again to the sounds made during straight coupling. You know . . . *gay-er.*

Manatees were long mistaken for mermaids and sirens—those feminine, boundary-crossing creatures who seduced sailors with their beauty and hypnotising songs. Their closest living relatives, incidentally, are hyraxes and elephants. Who could have guessed?

But beauty and mystery won't be enough to save this beautiful species. The West Indian manatees are endangered by hunting, pollution and collisions with boats and are down to 10,000 individuals in the wild. Tragically, without immediate action, they, and their raunchy sex lives, may very well soon go extinct.

RED DEER (*Cervus elaphus*)

Found: most of Europe, parts of western Asia, and central Asia. Parts of northwestern Africa. Introduced to South America and Australia

Length: up to 250 cm

Weight: up to 240 kg

Conservation status: least concern

Because yes, does can be lesbian, bi and they can be tops too.

Red deer are common across North Africa, Europe and Southwest Asia. They have a breeding season, aka "ruts," for about a month each year and during the rest of their time, mature adults live mostly in single sex groups. It's then, when they're not focused on breeding, that the does have a whole lot of gay sex.

It's pretty much the norm and about 70% of all does mate with each other outside the rut. Around a third play exclusively with other does and the rest are bi. They are divided more or less equally into tops ("mounters"), bottoms ("mountees") and versatiles. Occasionally when stags and does come together, it's the doe who tops the stag.

Both does and stags form pair bonds with members of their own sex and does in particular will travel great distances to be with their partner, calling to her until they're together again.

They also have some other fun gender stuff going on. Most females don't have antlers but some do. Most stags do but some don't. And the stags without antlers have been shown to be stronger and fitter.

Scientists, unsurprisingly, have either ignored these individuals or erased them as "statistical anomalies" (sound familiar?). Actually, of course, it's gender fluidity, gender nonconformity, maybe even another couple of genders. What it certainly isn't, is an anomaly.

Speaking of antlers…for red deer they are an erogenous zone and stags have been observed masturbating by rubbing their antlers against vegetation, sometimes getting hard and ejaculating in the process. Now you know.

EURASIAN OYSTERCATCHER (*Haematopus ostralegus*)

Found: western Europe, central Eurosiberia, Kamchatka, China, and the western coast of Korea

Length: up to 45 cm

Conservation status: near threatened

Oystercatchers are common shore birds across Europe. They often live in flocks and although most oystercatchers form monogamous pair bonds for breeding (you know, that story . . .), others have a very fun sex life.

Occasionally they get into a bisexual ménage à trois—two males with a female, or two females with a male—in which they all have an intimate relationship with each other. Females affectionately preen each other, males give each other courtship displays and all three have sex. These trios can last up to twelve years, aren't always exclusive, and members engage in hetero promiscuity outside the trio.

About 30% of oystercatcher populations are non-breeding, but just the same, they engage in sexual behaviour within and without their bonded pairs and trios. Females sometimes top males and it has been estimated that a straight pair will have sex 700 times during the breeding season. 700 times for one single clutch of eggs. For oystercatchers at least, sex is about much more than just breeding.

GIRAFFES (*Giraffa camelopardalis*)

Found: savannas and woodlands, ranging from Chad in the north to South Africa in the south, and from Niger in the west to Somalia in the east.

Height: up to 5.88 m tall

Weight: up to 1,192 kg

Conservation status: vulnerable

Few animals have filled as many children's picture books as the mighty giraffe. Little do those illustrators know how very gay they are.

Male giraffes have a unique form of flirting, and seduction, called necking. For up to an hour they'll stand next to each other, usually facing in opposite directions and gently rub their necks all over each other's bodies leading to erections all round and often orgasms. They might get excited enough to mount each other too, sometimes repeatedly and sometimes in groups of up to four or five. That's a lot of neck.

Giraffes are not big breeders—in fact only a small percentage of adults breed at all. In one study, during 3,200 hours of detailed study over an entire year, only one single straight mating was observed. In another study on the other hand, gay mounting and necking made up an impressive 94% of all giraffe sexual activity.

So next time you see a giraffe in a picture book or a commercial or on the cover of a magazine, just remember: super gay.

BONOBO (*Pan paniscus*)

Found: primary and secondary forests in the Congo Basin

Height: up to 115 cm

Weight: up to 60kg

Conservation status: endangered

If there is one species which stands alone as practically a queer superstar of the primate world it's the bonobo. This species, *Pan paniscus*—our closest living relative along with the chimpanzee—is endangered and lives only in a single area of the DRC. They have, as you may have heard, an incredibly raunchy sex life.

Almost all bonobos are bi and more than two thirds of female sex is with other females. Every couple of hours, a female engages in the wonderfully euphemistic "GG (genital-genital) rubbing" with other females.

The guys also get up to their fair share of gay fun. One of their favourite positions—known by the infinitely creative scientific community as "penis-fencing"—involves both partners hanging from a branch facing each other, swinging their hips and rubbing dicks. They also suck, and kiss with a lot of tongue. Males and females masturbate too, and males use inanimate objects for that purpose. And there are orgies. And from time to time they hook up with redtail monkeys (*Cercopithecus ascanius*)—a totally different species.

Sex is a defining point of bonobo life and is crucial for reconciliation and sharing, integrating new arrivals, forming coalitions and trade. They've even developed a set of hand signals to communicate what kind of fun they're up for including 25 gestures from "come over here and let's get it on" to "turn around" and "open your legs"—Grindr and OkCupid eat your heart out.

Most of these gestures are symbolic, but some are more abstract and some scientists think they represent the beginnings of complex language. The more sexual diversity, the more a species needs to communicate their desires. Enough said.

CHINSTRAP PENGUIN (*Pygoscelis antarcticus*)

Found: islands and shores in the Southern Pacific and the Antarctic Oceans

Height: up to 76 cm

Weight: up to 5.3 kg

Conservation status: least concern

Everyone loves penguins, but not everyone loves gay penguins.

Since at least 1911, penguins have been observed "engaging in homosexual behaviour." What's interesting is that the earliest report was considered too shocking, the behaviour too depraved, to be made public. Private copies of the report were written in Greek letters to keep them secret.

But the news got out. In the late 1990's, in a New York zoo, two male chinstrap penguins raised a chick. Roy and Silo became penguin superstars and their story was told in a play and at least two children's books. To this day, this small penguin family is being used as an argument by both North American liberals and the Christian right. Who knew that penguins could be so controversial?

QUEER PLANTS

Even though the scientific world has projected some very cis heteronormative illusions onto the plant world, the queerness of plants is inescapable. They can self-fertilize, cross-fertilize, be hermaphroditic, or not: they have a spectacular range of options and we're always discovering more about them.

Plants can work together with animals, fungi, and other plants for their pollen and seed distribution and they can alter their appearance dramatically in response to their environment.

Think of the spider plant growing on your windowsill. Remember that one time they had flowers? Sexual reproduction. Remember the ten million little babies you've given away to reluctant friends? Asexual clones. The clonal babies are genetically identical to the parent plant. Those new straggly spider plants now living on someone else's windowsill, with new stripes on their leaves and a different body shape depending on the light conditions; are they individuals now or just a distant part of the parent's body?

In June 2022, scientists discovered that a massive stretch of seagrass off the coast of Australia—big enough to cover three times the surface area of Manhattan—is actually *one single asexual individual* and the largest plant in the world.

And when we consider that a single species like "dandelion" can contain multitudes, our categories of species, community and individual are blurred forever. Honestly, we're here for it.

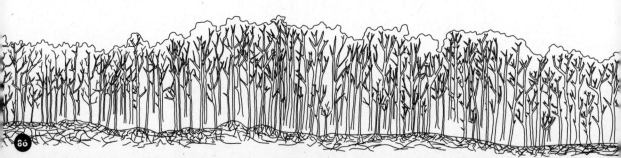

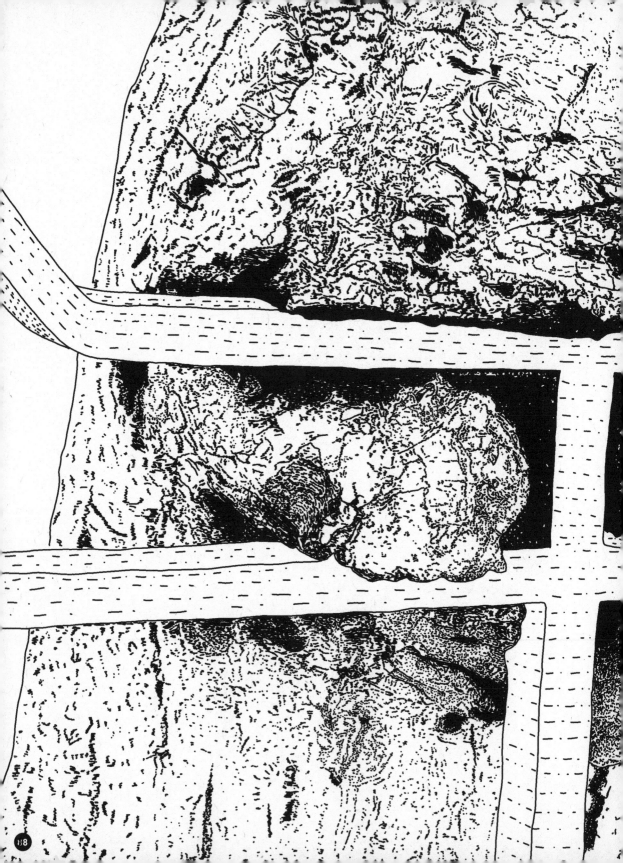

Tree, meet fence.
Adaptability in action!

AVOCADO TREE *(Persea americana)*

Found: cultivated in tropical and mediterranean climates. Native to
the Americas

Size: up to 20m in height

Conservation status: least concern

You know that avocados are really tasty. Did you know that they also sequentially dichogamous? They are!

Each cute little avocado flower is functionally male (pollen producing) and female (ovum producing) at different times of the day. All the flowers on a tree are of the same sex at the same time which is helpful to avoid self-pollination. They close up for a short break and open again with new sexual organs activated.

Also . . . yummy.

PRIMROSE (*Primula vulgaris*)

Found: native to western and southern Europe, northwest Africa, and parts of southwest Asia

Size: up to 30cm in height

Conservation status: least concern

Primroses have developed another solution to self-pollination. They have hermaphroditic flowers, but they have two different kinds—called pin and thrum—depending on the relative size and position, of parts of their flower (the stamens and pistils if you really must know).

Only pins and thrums can fertilize each other. Pins and pins don't get on, and thrums and thrums won't even make it to a second date.

Unless they're under stress—from habitat fragmentation in Belgium, for example, as the illustrator of this book discovered during their PhD research—in which case anything is possible.

Oh, and they're fucking beautiful.

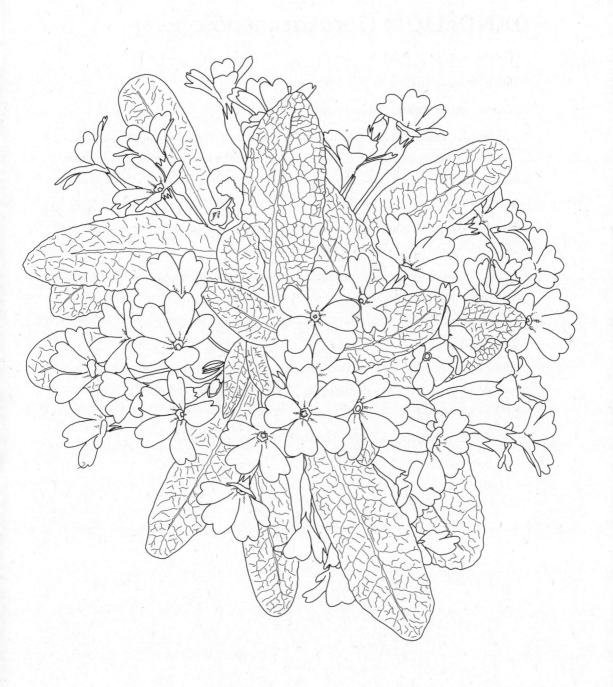

DANDELION (*Taraxacum officinale*)

Found: temperate regions

Size: flower heads 20-50mm across

Conservation status: least concern

For some, dandelions are the quintessential weeds, popping up through the cracks and making a mess of manicured lawns. For kids, they're known for their puffy little balls of seeds, fun to blow on and send their little parachutes flying. Less well known are their fun genetics.

In Europe, dandelions come in two types. One is sexual, like most seed plants, and has two sets of chromosomes. It can't self-fertilize.

The other is asexual with (usually) one extra set of chromosomes. This might be an adaptation for colonizing quickly in new habitats and in some places where dandelions have been introduced (the Americas for example), the asexual variety is dominant.

Just for extra complexity, the sexuals and asexuals can also hybridize with each other—leading to over 200 microspecies—and messing quite successfully with what we even mean by the word "species" anymore.

Dandelions: resilient, medicinal and wildly underappreciated.

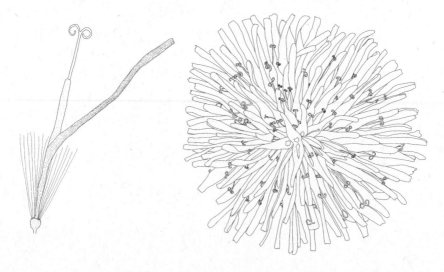

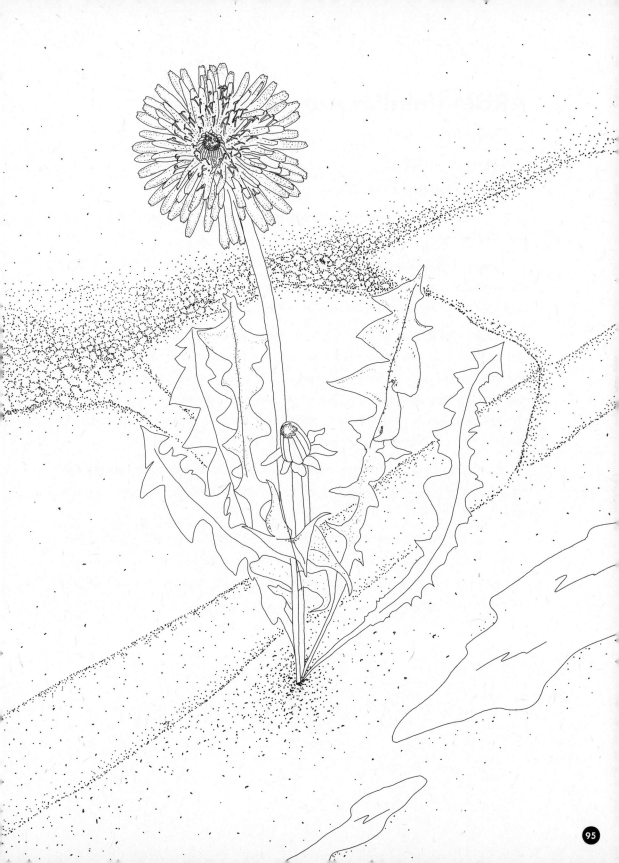

ARUM (family: *Araceae*)

Found: native to Europe, northern Africa, and western and central Asia

Size: up to 1m in height

Conservation status: depends on species

Arums are one of those flowering plants that just seem special when you see them. And they're hot!

Literally. They have a special form of respiration that heats up the flower to help release their scent into the world. For some species, humans for example, this smell is . . . unpleasant. One species is called dead-horse arum and for good reason.

But for flies it must be really interesting because they gather quickly—which is exactly what arums are after. They have a ring of hairs that trap the flies (and bees and other bugs) and dust them with pollen. Once they're finally released from the trap—which can take days—the flies go off and pollinate other arums. Arums are protogynous (female parts are ready before male parts) to avoid self-fertilization so they are dependent on the flies for sex to take place.

Employing animals to help out with sex is common for flowers but trapping them for days is pretty special. Heating up to make themselves more stinky, that's really special.

The Giant Arum is one of the largest—and stinkiest—flowers in the world. They flower for just a couple of days and the author and illustrator of this book were lucky enough to visit one together at a greenhouse on a flowering night. We can confirm: special, hot, and stinky.

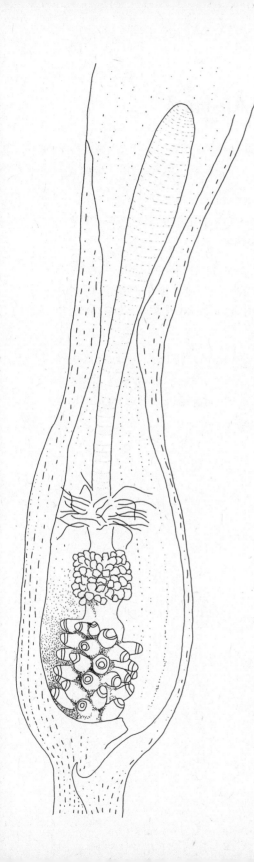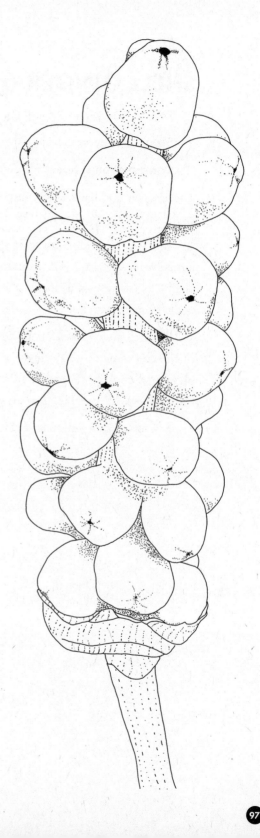

SHELL GINGER (genus: *Alpinia*)

Found: Asia, Australia, and the Pacific Islands

Size: varies by species

Conservation status: varies by species

These tropical gingers, like many flowering plants, are queer by their very nature. Every one of their gorgeous flowers is hermaphroditic.

But they have an extra edge. Self-pollination is a big problem and can lead to inbreeding. When a flower contains male and female parts, it can happen a lot. But Shell Gingers have developed a solution—they can actually move the sexual parts of their flowers around.

There are two kinds, defined by which parts they move and when. Over the course of the day some move through "male" phases (polleny bits exposed), and "female" phases (stigma exposed) while their counterparts do the opposite. Upon nightfall, all the flowers wither and the flower wiggling spectacle is over.

Scientists call it flexistyly, and it's cool.

Tropical ginger flowers

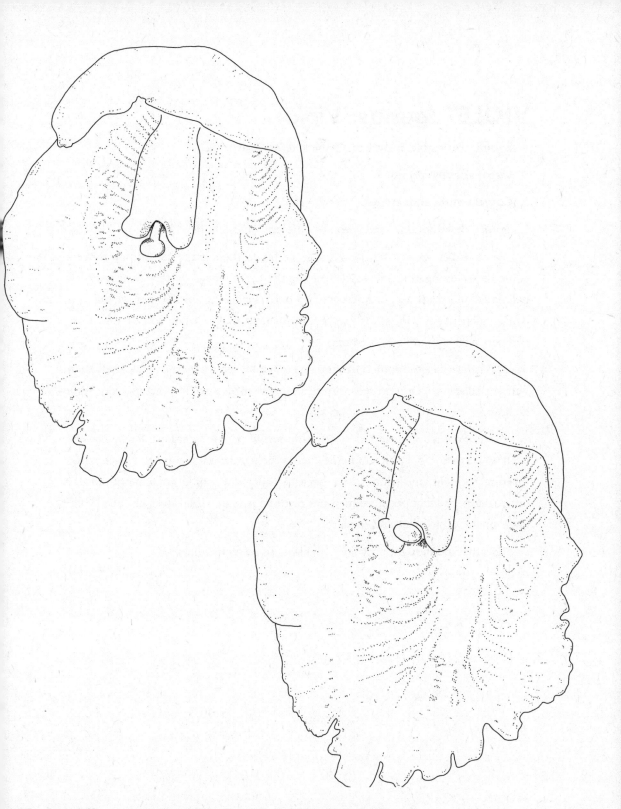

The two different positions of the "male" and "female" phases

VIOLET (genus: *Viola*)

Found: worldwide, mostly in northern temperate areas

Size: varies by species

Conservation status: least concern

It's good to have options. And if you're a violet, you might have a few.

Some violet species rely on flies to pollinate their gorgeous, showy flowers. Some have cleistogamous flowers, meaning that once they open they're already self-pollinated and ready to go. And some do both depending on the time of the year. Being independent with sex is useful for violets as they're often so tiny they don't compete well with other pollinators.

But help is nice too sometimes and several violet species recruit ants to help them with seed dispersal. Others explode to release their seeds up to five meters away. Some do both.

Pansies are a domesticated violet common in people's gardens. Pansy has also been used as a homophobic slur in the UK. As the word comes from the french *pensée,* meaning thought, and pansies have been considered a symbol of remembrance, it just makes sense that people sometimes plant pansies in public areas of cities where queerphobic attacks have taken place.

Creative and thought-provoking, pansies are perfectly queer.

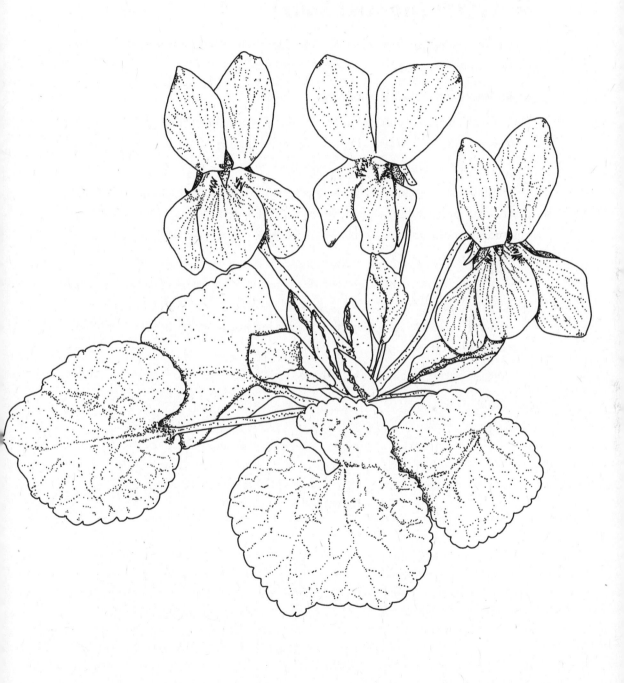

WILLOW (genus: *Salix*)

Found: mostly cold and temperate regions of the northern hemisphere

Size: varies by species

Conservation status: least concern

Willows are magical and are an important part of many cultural and religious traditions around the world. They also gave us aspirin which is definitely magic. Little known, though, is that they can change sex.

Willows are dioecious: they have male plants (with polleny catkins) and female plants (with ovary catkins). The research isn't published yet, but let's just say that a botanist we know observed a willow in their garden turning female after ten years of producing pollen.

They're great at hybridizing between species. That weeping willow you saw hanging over a pond once? It's a hybrid of one species from China and another from Europe. They're also really good at growing from cuttings or even just broken branches fallen on the ground.

Queerness and magic are everywhere.

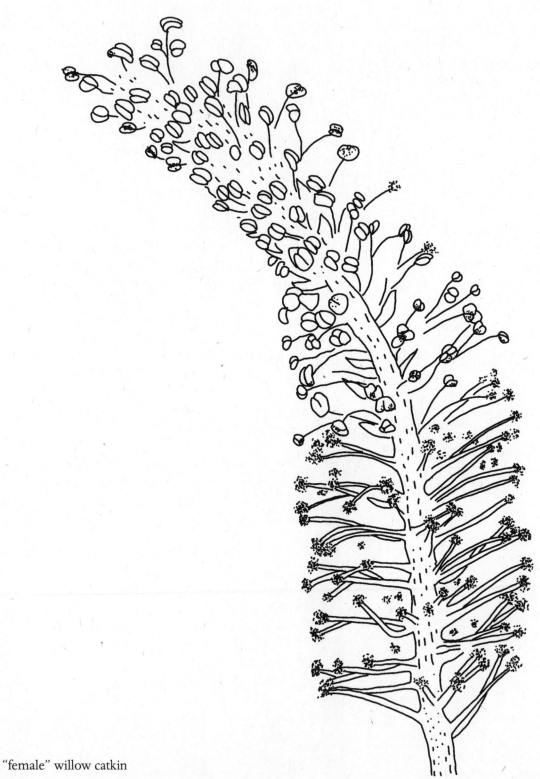

"female" willow catkin

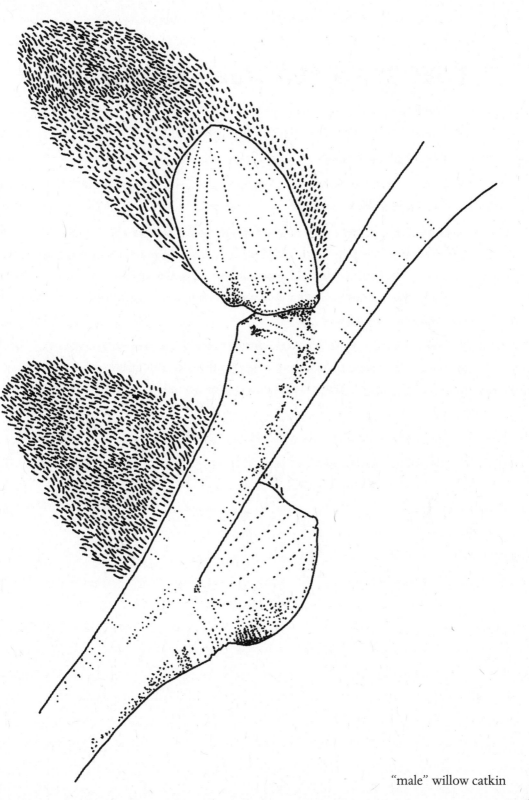

"male" willow catkin

EUROPEAN YEW *(Taxus baccata)*

Found: native to western, central, and southern Europe (including the British Isles), northwest Africa, northern Iran, and southwest Asia

Size: 10-20m in height

Conservation status: least concern, but endangered in some parts of their range by intensive land use

Truly ancient and highly toxic (at least to humans), this conifer has a few secrets. One giant tree called the Fortingall Yew lives in a graveyard in a Scottish village and might be 1,500 or 9000 years old depending who's guessing. Either way it's one of the oldest trees in Europe and has the widest trunk of any tree recorded in Britain. It's also slowly changing sex.

For as long as people have been writing about this ancient tree, it's been assumed to be male: producing pollen and not berries. But in 2015, on one small branch, the Fortingall Yew started producing bright red berries for all the world to see.

After several thousand years of just producing pollen.

Because it's never too late.

QUEER FUNGI

Y ou might not have thought about fungi a lot today. They might not seem like an especially important part of your life. But they live inside you, on you, all around you, everywhere.

The largest known organisms in the world are fungi—weighing hundreds of tons and spreading over 10 square kilometers. They can metabolize rocks and TNT. They live in the nuclear reactor in Chernobyl and might even be using the radioactivity there as a food source.

Their sex life is similarly complex—sexual, asexual, and sometimes both. One species has at least 20,000 different sexes.

And 90% of plant species depend on them for survival. In the body of a single plant there can be hundreds of species living threaded between cells protecting the plant from disease. Plant life wouldn't exist as we know it without mycorrhizal symbiosis—the underground interconnection of plants and fungi that has existed for at least 400 million years.

With such intimacy, where do trees end and fungi begin? Our bodies are full of fungi too and they fundamentally change who we are. Life is complex, categories are fuzzy. We're into it.

Beech mushrooms, an edible mushroom native to South-East Asia

SPLIT GILL MUSHROOM (*Schizophyllum commune*)

Found: worldwide

Size: caps are 1-4cm across

Conservation status: least concern

You may not have heard about this fungus, but you really should get to know them if you enjoy diversity. They grow all over the world, except Antarctica, and might be one of the most widespread fungi in the world. They like to eat wood and their tasty (to some) little mushrooms pop up after the rain.

Oh, and they have no less than 23,328 sexes.

Some even say 28,000.

A lot, at any rate.

Strictly speaking, they're not sexes in the animal sense, but mating types—they have two points in their genetic structure that come in different forms, leading to this staggering variation. Other fungi have multiple mating types too, but this creative little mushroom might be the most diverse. More mating types means less inbreeding, which means greater genetic diversity and might explain why *Schizophyllum commune* is doing so well.

Unlike animals, many fungi can bump a bit of their body into another fungus's body and exchange genes. Which is sexy and convenient. For split gills, while not every combination is fertile, each mating type still has 22,960 possible mates, so the chances of bumping into someone compatible are very good. Which must make using dating apps a whole lot easier.

FLY AGARIC (*Amanita muscaria*)

Found: Worldwide, native to conifer and deciduous woodlands throughout the temperate and boreal regions of the Northern Hemisphere

Size: caps are 8-20cm in diameter

Conservation status: least concern

Probably the most iconic species of toadstool, fly agarics are great for sitting on if you're a gnome or a fairy. They're also good for scoring points in video games. They're psychoactive and used traditionally by Indigenous shamans in Siberia and elsewhere. They pop up in *Alice in Wonderland* and can cause Alice in Wonderland Syndrome—perceptual disorders that make things seem larger or smaller than they are. Yes, really.

But is this species a species at all? Genetic studies have shown that *Amanita muscaria* contains multiple varieties, some genetically different enough to be considered species. So this species is more a species *complex*, a group of closely related organisms so similar in appearance that the boundaries between them can end up unclear. Blurring boundaries and messing with definitions, that's queer enough for us.

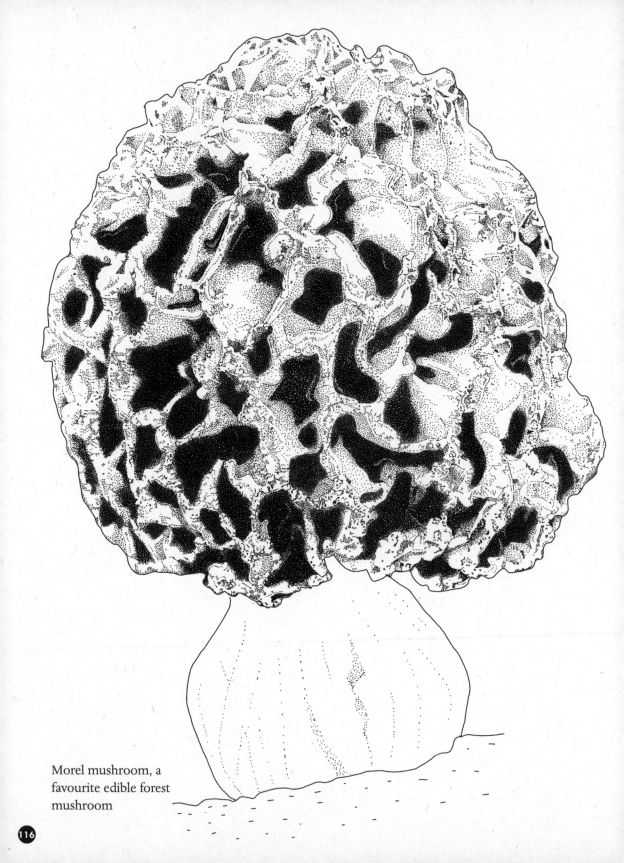

Morel mushroom, a
favourite edible forest
mushroom

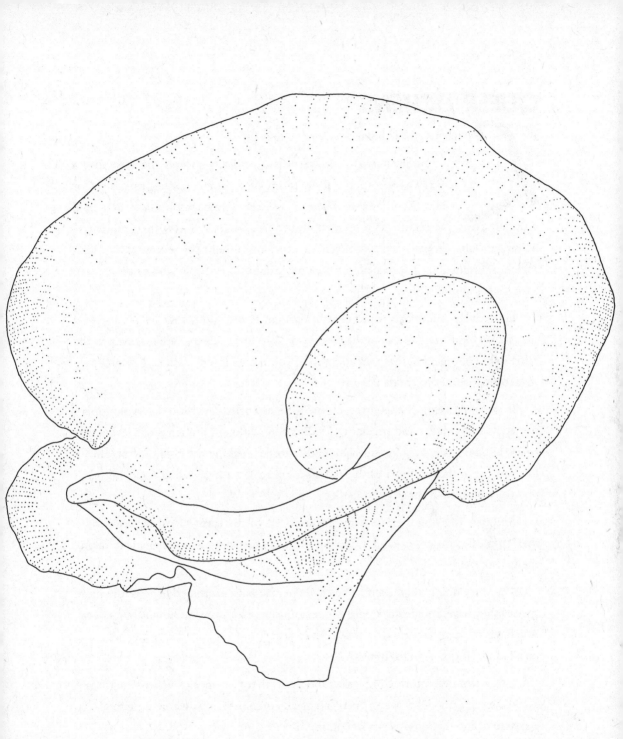

Oyster mushroom, another well known edible mushroom

QUEER LICHENS

Lichens smash binaries wherever they go.

Symbiosis was once seen as a radical concept: the idea that a lichen was a compound organism of a fungus and a green alga (or a photosynthesizing bacteria called cyanobacteria) that benefited mutually from the relationship seemed absurd to scientists. Surely the fungus was holding the alga captive and exploiting it for its photosynthetic super powers. Working together? Impossible! Those ideas say a lot more about the people who believed them than it does about lichens.

Fungal-algal symbiosis *is* pretty wild though. Fungi and plants are far apart on the tree of life. Fungi and cyanobacteria (who also form lichens) are not even in the same domain, meaning that you and a mushroom are closer relations than any two that come together to create lichens.

In general, living things diverge over time as each branch of the evolutionary tree splits into smaller and smaller twigs. But here, different branches come together again, known as convergence: a plant and a fungus making a whole new organism. I can photosynthesize but I can't eat rocks. Oh really? I love eating rocks but can't photosynthesize—want to get together some time?

And they're living their best life, covering 8% of the earth's land surface—more than tropical rainforests—and surviving in space, just because humans love taking things into space.

The story doesn't end there. The closer people have examined lichens, the more species they have found mixed into the relationship. Not just one fungus but several. And loads of bacteria turned up who couldn't eat rocks or photosynthesize but could do all kinds of other useful things.

It's grown ever more complex to the point that two-species lichens might not even be a thing and what we've been calling an "organism" this whole time might be a system of interactions—a whole community.

Lichens. Bringing all the complexity and we love them for it.

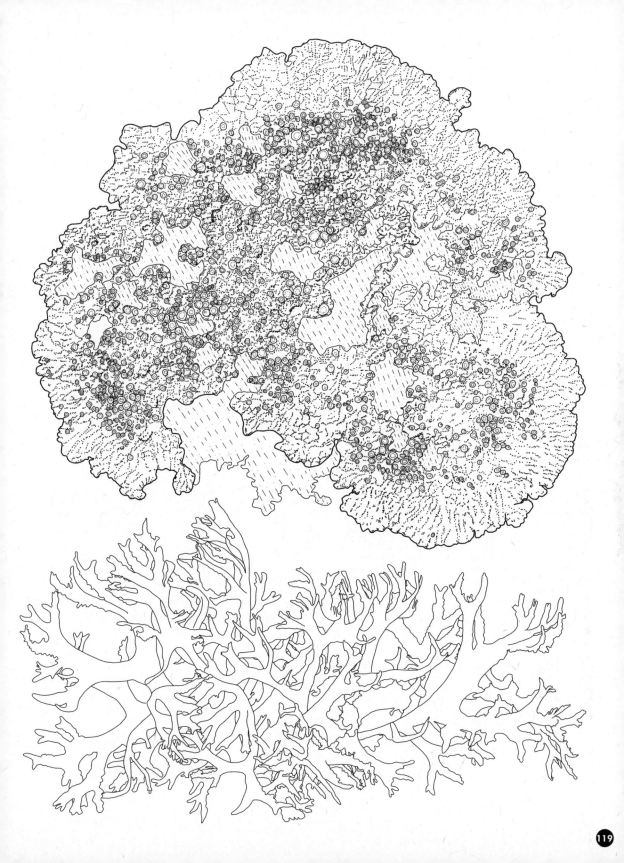

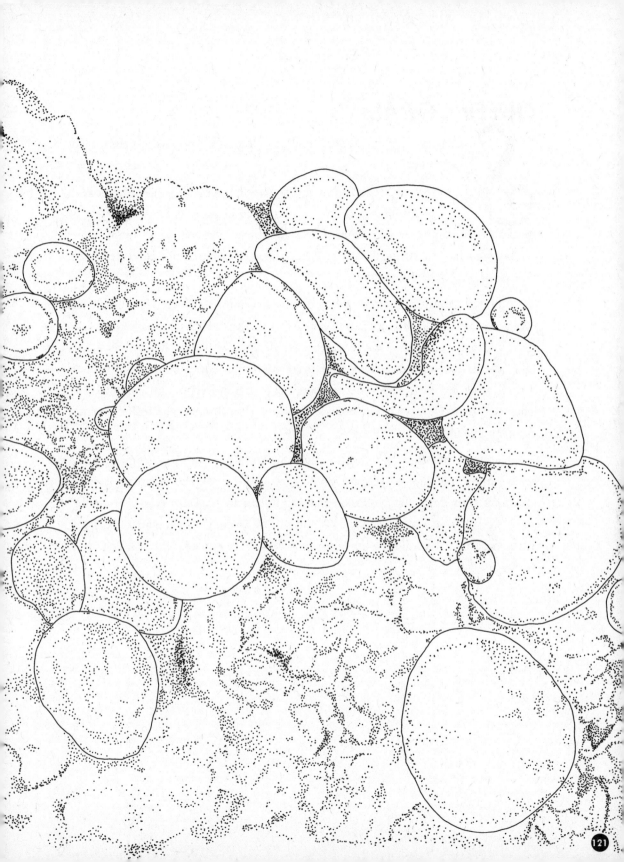

QUEER CORAL

Symbiosis is a foundational concept of ecology. And, like lichens, corals are all over it.

They might not look it at first glance, but corals are little animals— just a few milimeters across, living together in a colony. A coral reef is the result of them excreting calcium carbonate to create a skeleton to live in. They can be gonochoristic (when a coral polp has one sex), or hermaphroditic. They can reproduce sexually and asexually.

But they don't do it alone. They usually live intimately with dinoflagellates ("whirling whips") who are even smaller and can photosynthesize (we can think of them as micro-algae but they aren't actually plants. It's complicated). Like lichens, there's a mutual benefit to this relationship. Thanks for this nice place to live and some carbon dioxide—here, have some solar powered energy and nutrients. There are also viruses, bacteria, archaea, and fungi in the mix just to keep things complex and interesting.

These relationships can break down under stress. With changing water temperatures and salinity levels, the dinoflaggelates are expelled, which leads to coral bleaching. Climate change, pollution and over-fishing are major threats—10% of the world's corals have already died and 60% are at risk. Occupying less than 0.1% of the Earth's ocean area, coral reefs are home to at least 25% of marine species. Their loss is a tragedy for us all.

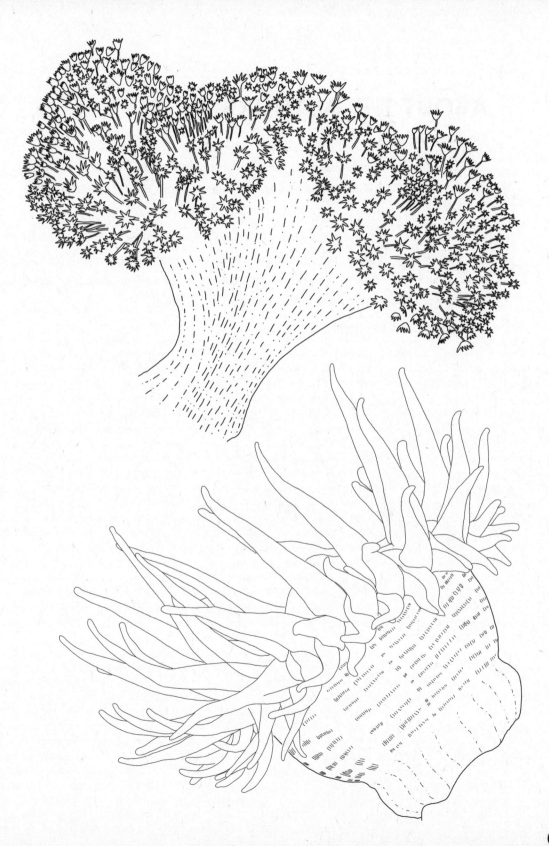

ABOUT THE AUTHORS

Kes Otter Lieffe

Kes Otter Lieffe is a working class, chronically ill, femme, trans woman. She is an author, teacher and community organizer currently based near Berlin. Kes is the author of a trilogy of trans feminist novels and several short stories.

A grassroots community organizer for over two decades, Kes has worked and organized in Europe, the Middle-East, and Latin America. Her work focuses particularly on the intersection of gender, queerness and environmental struggles and creating radical alternatives to the trash-fire of capitalism.

Find out more at otterlieffe.com

Anja Van Geert

After completing a PhD in Plant Ecology, Anja Van Geert has been part of many ecological projects and adventures including growing herbs at an urban farm in their home town of Brussels. They currently live at a farm in the south west of Scotland with their partner Emma and their cats Moisey and Peanut.

Find out more at pinprimrose.co.uk

SUBSCRIBE!

For as little as $13 / month, you can
support a small, independent publisher
and get every book that we publish—
delivered to your doorstep!

www.Microcosm.Pub/BFF